Which Toy for Which Child

A Consumer's Guide for Selecting Suitable Toys

U.S. Consumer Product Safety Commission
Washington, D.C. 20207

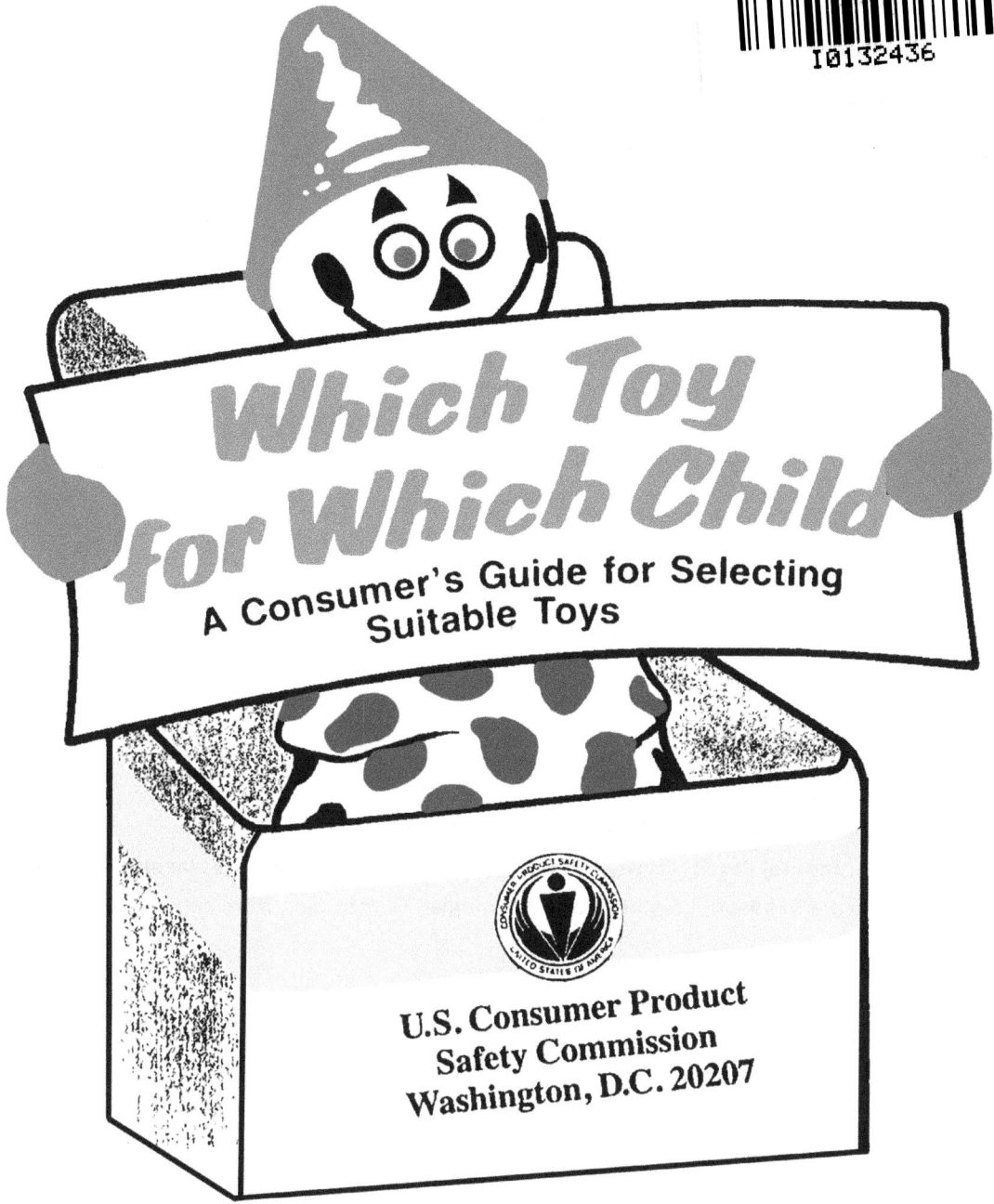

AGES BIRTH THROUGH FIVE

PUB. NO. 285

Developed under Contract CPSC-C-85-1089 by Dr. Barbara Goodson, Developmental Psychologist, Abt Associates, Inc. Cambridge, Massachusetts and Dr. Martha Bronson, Educational Psychologist, Cambridge, Massachusetts

ISBN 978-0-9825854-6-7

Digitally Reproduced in 2010
CONVERPAGE
23 Acorn Street
Scituate, MA 02066
781-378-1996

WHICH TOY FOR WHICH CHILD.

Play **is a natural activity** for every young child. Play provides many opportunities for children to learn and grow – physically, mentally and socially. If play is the child's work then toys are the child's tools, and appropriate toys can help children do their work well.

Young children explore objects in their environment by "mouthing" them. Children can choke to death on such items. These items include toys (such as balloons and small balls), and household and food items (such as hot dogs, peanuts, popcorn, coins, batteries, etc.) Although toys intended for young children should be free of small parts that could cause a chocking incident, toys intended for older children may find their way into the hands of younger children. **Reminder: Be sure to keep ALL small items out of the hands of children who mouth objects, especially children under the age of three. Remind three and four year olds to keep such items out of their mouths. Instruct older children to keep these items out of reach of younger children.**

This booklet offers suggestions for selecting suitable toys for children birth to 5 years of age. It was prepared by the U.S. Consumer Product Safety Commission, the government agency that is charged with protecting the public against unreasonable risks of injury associated with consumer products.

A **parent or friend** choosing a toy for a child must consider several things. A good toy should be:

- Safe for that child's age, well constructed, and durable;
- Appealing and interesting to the child;
- Suited to the child's physical capabilities, and;
- Suited to the child's mental and social development

This booklet provides some guidelines to help in selecting toys that meet these criteria. The suggestions in the booklet are based on three sources. (1) review of reference works on child development, (2) observations of children at play, and (3) product analysis of toys to determine which characteristics are most critical in defining the appropriate ages of the intended users.

T **his booklet** is organized in the following way. Brief outlines of children's' **ABILITIES AND INTERESTS** are followed by categorized **TOY LISTS** for each of five age groups.

The five age groups are

- Young infants (birth to 6 months)
- Older infants (7 to 12 months)
- Young toddlers (1 year olds)
- Older toddlers (2 year olds)
- Preschoolers (ages 3, 4 and 5)

ABILITIES AND INTERESTS sections list physical, mental and social abilities and interests for each age that are particularly relevant to selecting appropriate toys. Note that these lists indicate average development – the age range at which the "average" child can be expected to achieve a particular skill or develop a specific interest. The ages in the text are only approximate. Children develop skills at uneven rates – any one child may be "above average: in one skill and "below average" in another skill. For an individual child, the parent is the best judge of the child's abilities and interests at any point in his or her development, and should select toys suitable for that child's profile of capabilities.

TOY LIST sections give toy suggestions in six major categories with subcategories under each to help in finding a particular toy type. The major categories and subcategories are listed on the following page. Note that these sections do not constitute a comprehensive list of all toy products that might be suitable for a particular age. They do suggest general toy types suitable for that age group. This booklet does **not** judge The play value or benefits of specific toys. For example, suitable types of projectile toys are described in the **TOY LISTS**, Although the potential safety hazards of these toys lead many in the field to recommend against them.

ALL TOYS (general category orienting the consumer to special features of toys that are relevant to the particular age group).

ACTIVE PLAY
   Push and Pull Toys
   Ride-On Toys
   Outdoor and Gym Equipment
   Sports Equipment

MANIPULATIVE PLAY
   Constructions Toys
   Puzzles
   Pattern-Making Toys
   Manipulative Toys
   Dressing, Lacing and Stringing Toys
   Sand and Water Play Toys

MAKE-BELIEVE PLAY
   Dolls
   Stuffed Toys
   Puppets
   Role Play Scenes
   Play Scenes
   Transportation Toys
   Projectile Toys

CREATIVE PLAY
   Musical Instruments
   Art and Craft Materials
   Audio-Visual Equipment

LEARNING PLAY
   Games
   Specific Skill Development Toys
   Books

TOY SAFETY. Major areas of consideration to all toys are safety and durability. Toys should be constructed to withstand the uses and abuses of children in the age range for which the toy is appropriate.

The U.S. Consumer Product Safety Commission (CPSC) has safety regulations for certain toys. Manufacturers must design and manufacture their products to meet these regulations so that hazardous products are not sold. In addition, many toy manufacturers also adhere to the toy industry's voluntary safety standards.

WHAT THE GOVERNMENT DOES
Mandatory Toy Safety Regulations

For All Ages

- No shock or thermal hazards in electrical toys
- Amount of lead in toy paint severely limited
- No toxic materials in or on toys
- Art materials that are used by children under 12 should be non-hazardous and should indicate they confirm with ASTM D-4236
- Latex balloons and toys and games with latex balloons must be labeled warning of the choking and suffocation hazards associated with pieces of and uninflated balloons

Under Age 3

- Unbreakable – will withstand use and abuse
- No small parts or pieces which could become lodged in the throat
- Infant rattles large enough not to become lodged in child's throat and constructed so as not to separate into small pieces
- No balls with diameters 1.75 inches of less

For Ages 3 through 6

- All toys and games with small parts must be labeled to warn of the choking hazard to young children

For 3 years and older

- The following toys must be labeled to warn of the choking hazard to young children
- All balls and toys and games with balls with a diameter 1.75 inches of less, and
- All marbles and toys and games with marbles

Under Age 8

- No electrically operated toys with heating elements
- No sharp points on toys
- No sharp edges on toys.

CPSC also can remove from the marketplace toys presenting hazards not covered by the regulations.

What the Industry Does: Voluntary Standard for Toy Safety

- Puts age and safety labels on toys
- Puts warning labels on crib gyms advising that they be removed from the crib when babies can push up on hands and knees to prevent strangling
- Makes squeeze toys and teethers large enough not become lodged in an infant's throat
- Assures that the lid of a toy chest will stay open in any position to which it is raised and not fall unexpectedly on a child.
- Limits string length on crib and play pen toys to reduce the risk of strangulations

What a Parent Can Do

Reduce Choking Risk

- Look for and read age and safety labels. Any toy that is age labeled for children three years and older should be kept away from children under the age of three – such toys **may** have small parts and **could** cause choking if placed in the mouth
- Keep uninflated balloons and broken balloon pieces away from children

- Rounded and oval objects (e.g. balls, marbles, etc.) that fit easily into a child's mouth may be difficult to remove from a throat and cause choking

Reduce Strangulation Risk

- Crib toys with strings, cords, ribbons, etc. (used to hang toys across a crib or to the side of a crib) present a strangulation risk when babies are just starting to push up on hands and knees, usually about 5 months of age. **REMOVE ALL CRIB TOYS WHICH ARE STRUNG ACROSS CRIB OR PLAYPEN AREA WHEN BABIES BEGIN TO PUSH UP ON HANDS AND KNEES OR ARE 5 MOMTHS OF AGE, WHICHEVER OCCURS FIRST.**

General Toy Safety

- Keep toys intended for older children away from younger children – such toys may injure young children
- Check all toys periodically for breakage and potential hazards – damaged or dangerous toys should be repaired or thrown away immediately
- Store toys safety --- teach children to put toys away so they are not tripping hazards, check toy boxes and shelves for safety

<u>For further information write to the:</u>

U.S. Consumer Product Safety Commission
Washington, D C 20207
To report a toy related complaint, call the toll-free
hotline: 1-800-638-CPSC

Where to Find Toys Suitable For Your Child:

- If your child is an infant age 6 months or younger go to page **10**
- If your child is an infant between 7 and 12 months, go to page **17**
- If your child is a 1 year old, go to page **25**
- If your child is a 2 year old, go to page **35**
- If your child is a preschooler age 3, 4 or 5 years go to page **45**

Young Infants 0 to 6 Months

ABILITIES AND INTERESTS

PHYSICAL

- Visual focus matures – follows objects with eyes
- Learns to localize sounds and turns to see
- Gains control of hands – learns to bat, then reach and grasp objects
- Discovers feet, - brings feet to mouth and explores with feet
- Begins to sit with support
- Large muscle play may include rolling, scooting, rocking, bouncing

MENTAL

- Explores world with eyes and ears and begins to explore with hands and feet and mouth
- Enjoys creating effects in the environment by own actions
- Begins to recognize familiar people objects and events – then to anticipate them
- Becomes aware of novelty and strangeness in people objects and events

- Develops definite preferences for certain people, objects and events
- May imitate simple movements if in own repertoire
- Does one thing at a time

SOCIAL

- Special interest in people (faces and voices especially)
- Begins to smile at faces, voices and mirror image
- Quits crying when sees face or hears voice
- Begins to seek attention and contact with people
- Distinguishes among familiar people and has preferences
- Begins to coo and gurgle, babble and laugh aloud, play with sounds
- Listens to voices and may imitate sounds already in own repertoire

ALL TOYS

Toys for this age are primarily for looking, listening, sucking or fingering.

Infants 0-2 months enjoy seeing and hearing interesting things.

Infants 2-6 months show growing interest in touching, holding batting turning, shaking, kicking, mouthing and tasting objects.

Infants like to see:
- Bright primary colors

- High contrast
- Simple designs
- Clear lines and features
- Human face features (especially eyes)
- Bulls eye pattern

Infants enjoy watching hanging objects or "mobiles" that move by wind, wind-up action or infant's own activity

Toys for watching should be suspended only 8-14 inches (200-360mm) from the infant's eyes and angled toward his/her eyes, then moved up out of reach when he/she can touch them

Toys for watching are more appealing if they move and make noise (but movement should be slow and noise not too loud or sudden

Infants enjoy variety

Infants enjoy producing effects on toys by their own activity

Toys for holding should be light and easy to grasp

Mouthable toys should have **all safety features** recommended for infants

- No sharp points or edges
- No small parts to be lodged in throat, ears, nose
- No electrical parts
- Nontoxic materials
- No glass or brittle plastic
- No parts to entrap fingers, toes, hands
- No long strings

ACTIVITY PLAY

Outdoor or Gym Equipment – infant swings with adult supervision

Sports Equipment
From about 6-9 weeks

- Clutch balls
- Texture balls
- Soft squeeze balls

(All balls given to this age group should be at least 1-3/4 inches (44 mm) in diameter, however if any object appears to fit easily in the child's mouth, **keep it away from the child.)**

MANIPULATIVE PLAY

Construction Toys

From about 4 months – soft blocks

Manipulative Toys

From 6-8 weeks

- Simple rattles
- Teethers
- Light, sturdy cloth toys
- Squeeze toys
- Toys suspended above or to the side of infant for batting and grasping

From about 4 months

- Disks, keys on ring
- Interlocking plastic rings
- Small hand-held manipulables

- Toys on suction cups
- Crib gyms (children who can push up on hands and knees can strangle on crib gyms – be sure to remove crib gym from crib or playpen at this time).

MAKE-BELIVE PLAY

Dolls

- Soft baby dolls, soft bodied dolls, or rag dolls – all with molded (not loose) hair

Stuffed Toys

- Small plush animals
- Music box animals (operated and monitored for safety by adults)
- Grab-on soft toys

Puppets

- Soft hand puppets (held and moved by adults)

Role-Play Materials

- Mirrors (large, unbreakable) fastened to crib, playpen or wall (peak interest in mirrors 4-6 months)

CREATIVE PLAY (arts, crafts, music)

Audio-Visual Equipment (Adult Operated)
- Records, tapes or CD's (gentle regular rhythms, lullabies.)
- Music boxes

LEARNING PLAY

Books

May enjoy listening to a story being read.

Older Infants 7 to 12 Months
ABILITIES AND INTERESTS

PHYSICAL
- Begins to sit alone
- Begins to creep and crawl onto or into things
- Begins to pull to a stand, cruise (walk holding furniture), and walk alone (10-16 months).
- Interest in moving about and practicing motor skills
- Develops "pincer" (thumb and finger) grasp and begins to hold objects with one hand while manipulating them with the other
- With objects wants to bag, insert, poke, twist, squeeze, drop, shake, bite, throw, open/shut, push/pull, empty/fill, drag along
- Enjoys bath play – kicking and splashing

MENTAL
- Interest in appearing and disappearing (objects and people) develops "object permanence" (looks for object out of sight at approximately 11 months
- Interest in container/contained relationship – likes to empty cupboards, drawers and containers of objects
- Interest in letting go and dropping objects (will use string to pull back vanished objects).
- Interest in exploration and likes many objects to explore.
- Likes to operate simple mechanisms (open-shut, push/pull) and create effects

- Remembers people, objects, games, actions with toys shows persistence and interest in novelty
- Beginning interest in picture books

SOCIAL

- May fear strangers or react to change – plays best with familiar person nearby
- Watches and may imitate others
- Sensitive to social approval and disapproval
- Interest in getting attention and creating social effects
- Enjoys simple social games "peek-a-boo," "bye-bye"
- Babbles and plays with language – may try to imitate sounds
- Recognizes own name and may begin to point to named objects or obey simple commands

ALL TOYS

Infants 7-9 months interested in longer and more extensive exploration of toys. Infants of this age like to:

- Bang
- Insert
- Poke
- Twist
- Squeeze
- Drop
- Shake
- Bite
- Throw
- Open and shut
- Empty and fill

Infants 10-12 months show beginning interest in object mastery and like many objects to explore. Infants of this age like:

- Stacking
- Putting in and taking out
- Pouring out
- Fitting one object into another
- Opening and closing
- Pressing levers
- Turning things (not unscrewing yet)
- Pushing balls and cars

Generally infants in this age range are interested in:

- Operating simple mechanisms
- Containers and the container/contained relationship
- Appearing and disappearing objects

At earlier ages infants enjoy producing effects by their own actions

Toys for infants:

- Safe for mouthing
- Non-toxic materials
- No sharp points or edges
- Non breakable, no glass or brittle plastic
- No small parts to be lodged in throat, ears, nose
- No parts to entrap fingers, toes and hands
- No long strings

ACTIVE PLAY

Push and Pull Toys

Push toys without rods (simple cars, animals on wheels or rollers)

Outdoor or Gym Equipment

Infant swings (with adult supervision). Soft low climbing platform for crawlers

Sports Equipment

Transparent balls
Chime balls
Flutter balls
Actions balls

(All balls given to this age group should be at least 1-3/4 inches (44 mm) in diameter, however, if any object appears to fit easily in the child's mouth **keep it away from the child**.)

MANIPULATIVE PLAY

Construction Toys
Soft blocks
Rubber blocks
Rounded wood blocks

Puzzles
From about 10 months
Brightly colored, lightweight crib and and playpen puzzles (2-3 pieces).

Manipulative Toys

- Teethers
- Light sturdy cloth toys

- Toys on suction cups
- Small, hand-held manipulables
- Disks/keys on rings
- Squeeze-squeak toys
- Roly-poly toys
- Activity boxes and cubes
- Pop-up boxes (easy operation
- Containers with object to empty and fill
- Large rubber or plastic pop beads
- Simple nesting cups
- Stacking ring cones (few rings and safe stick).
- Graspable (unbreakable) mirror toys which can be held and played with
- Loses interest in crib gyms and toys suspended above when can sit up and move about (crib gyms can create a strangulation hazard, stop using when child can push up on hands and knees at about 5 months

Sand and Water Play Toys

- Activity boxes for bath
- Simple floating toys

MAKE-BELIEVE PLAY

Dolls

- Soft baby dolls, soft-bodied dolls, or rag dolls – all with molded (not loose) hair

Stuffed Toys

- Small plush animals
- Music box animals (operated and monitored for safety by adult)
- Grab or soft toys

- Big soft toys for hugging and roughhousing

Puppets

- Soft hand puppets – child may handle but must be operated as puppets by adult

Role Play Materials

- Low wall-mounted mirrors to see self sit, creep, crawl, etc.

Transportation Toys

- Simple push cars (one-piece).

CREATIVE PLAY (arts, crafts, music)

Musical Instrument

- Rubber or wood blocks that rattle or tinkle

Art and Craft Materials (from about 12 months)

- Large paper
- Large crayons for scribbling

AUDIO-VISUAL EQUIPMENT (Adult Operated)

- Records, tapes of CDs (simple songs, lullabies, music with simple rhythms).
- Music boxes

LEARNING PLAY

Books

- Cloth books
- Plastic books
- Small cardboard books

(Note: Some children enjoy "lap reading" (being read to) from this age onward. When adult-held, paper picture books are appropriate.

YOUNG TODDLERS (1 YEAR OLDS)

ABILITIES AND INTERESTS

PHYSICAL

- Endless exercise of physical skills
- Likes to lug, dump, push, pull, pile, knock down, empty and fill
- Lies to climb – can manage small indoor steps
- Manipulation is more exploratory than skillful
- Active interest in multiple small objects
- By 2 years, can kick, catch a large ball
- By 2 years, can string large beads, turn knob, use screw motion (All beads given to this age group should be at least 1-3/4 inches (44 mm) in diameter. However, if any object appears to fit easily in the child's mouth, **keep it away from the child)**

MENTAL

- Interest in causing effects
- Interest in mechanisms and objects that move or can be moved – prefers action toys
- Combines objects with other objects – makes simple block structures, uses simple stacking toys, does simple puzzles
- Very curious – constant experimentation with objects
- Interest in hidden-object toys
- At 1-1/2 to 2 years, groups/matches similar objects – enjoys simple sorting toys

- Identifies objects by pointing – can identify pictures in book
- Enjoys water, sand play
- Makes marks on paper, scribbles spontaneously

SOCIAL

- Most solitary play – relates to adults better than to children
- Tries to do adult tasks
- Expresses affection for others - shows preference for certain soft toys, dolls
- Likes being read to, looking at picture books, likes nursery rhymes
- By 1 1/2 , enjoys interactive games such as tag

ALL TOYS

Children prefer action toys, toys that produce movement or sounds by child's own efforts

- Toys need not be highly detailed but should be realistic looking
- Toys should be lightweight for easy lifting, carrying
- Bright colors preferred

In play child always on the move – large muscle activities such as running, climbing dominate of small muscle activities such as exploring objects, constructing.

Child beginning to combine, put together objects

Beginning of imitative play

Toys should meet safety regulations for age

- Sturdy, unbreakable, not likely to break into small pices and strong enough for child to stand on or in
- Nontoxic materials
- No sharp points or edges
- Too large to be lodged in windpipe, ears, nostrils
- No detachable small parts
- No parts that could pinch or entrap fingers, toes, hair
- Not put together with easily exposed straight pins, sharp wires, nails.
- No electrical parts, unless supervised by adult

ACTIVE PLAY

Push and Pull Toys

- Push toys with rods (rods with large handles on ends)
- Toys to push on floor – simple, sturdy with large wheels
- Special noise and action effects
- For steady walkers pull toys on strings (broad-based to tip less easily)

From about 1 ½

- Simple doll carriages
- Wagons – low open big enough for child to get in
- Small rocking horses – confined rocking arc, stout handles rather than reins, knee height on child
- Push/pull toys filled with multiple objects

Ride-On Toys

- Ride-ons propelled by pushing with feet – no pedals
- Stable ride-ons – 4 or more wheels, wheels spaced wide apart, child's feet flat on floor when seated
- Ride-ons with storage bins
- Ride-ons that make noise, look like animals

Outdoor and Gym Equipment

- All gym equipment needs adult supervision
- Low, soft climbing platforms
- Tunnels for crawling swings (pushed by adult) – seats curved or body shaped of energy absorbing material with restraining strap

From about 1 ½

- Simple, low climbing structures
- Low slides with handrails
- Outdoor play equipment with stationary rather than moving parts

Sports Equipment

- Soft light weight balls, especially with interesting visual effects, noises, unpredictable movement
- Chime ball, flutter ball
- Large balls (easier for child to maneuver)

(All balls given to this age group should be at least 1-3/4 inches (44mm) in diameter. However, if any object appears to fit easily in the child's mouth **keep it away from the child**)

MANIPULATIVE PLAY

Construction Toys

- Small lightweight stacking blocks (15-25 pieces).

Before 1-1/2 most interlocking mechanisms are too difficult

From around 1-1/2

- Solid wooden unit blocks (20-40)
- Large hollow building blocks
- Large plastic blocks (204 inches or 50-100 mm) to press together

Puzzles

- Simple pre-puzzles or form boards – 2-3 pieces each piece a familiar shape

From around 1-1/2

3-5 piece puzzles with knobs easier to use (knobs firmly attached)

Pattern-Making Toys

Peg board with a few large pegs

Manipulative Toys

- Activity boxes attached to crib or playpen or freestanding – simple action mechanisms (doors, lids, switches).
- Hidden object toys
- Simple pop-up toys operated by pushing a button or knob
- Nesting cups – round shape few pieces
- Simple stacking toys – few pieces no order necessary
- Shape sorters – a few common shapes

From around 1-1/2

- Fit together toys of about 5 pieces
- Activity boxes and more complex action mechanisms – turning knob or dial, turning simple key

- Pounding/hammering toys
- Nesting toys – square or other shapes
- Stacking toys to 4-5 pieces
- Simple matching toys
- Simple number/counting boards (1-5) with large pegs
- Simple lock boxes and lock/key toys
- Jack-in-the-box toys (adult supervision if toys spring back quickly).
- Toys with screwing action (child can usually ménage only 1 turn

Dressing, Lacing, Stringing Toys

- Large colored beads (fewer than 10) (All balls given to this age group should be at least 1-3/4 inches (44mm) in diameter however, if any object appears to fit easily in the child's mouth **keep it away from the child)**

From around 1-1/2

- Nesting tub toys
- Bathtub activity centers
- Funnels, colanders
- Small sandbox tools(rake should have blunt teeth)

MAKE BELIEVE PLAY

Dolls

- Soft-bodied or all-rubber baby dolls
- Simple dolls with no hair, moving eyes, or movable limbs
- Dolls to fit easily in child's arms, or small dolls (5-6 inches)
- Simple accessories for caretaking – bottle, blanket
- Simple doll c
- clothes, need not be detachable

From around 1-1/2

- large peg people

Stuffed Toys

- Very soft lightweight easy to hold.
- Slender limbs on toys for easy grasp
- For safety reasons, no whiskers, buttons, bows or bells

Puppets

- Puppets operated by adult

From around 1-1/2

- Small hand puppets sized to fit child's hand
- Soft, plush puppets that double as stuffed toys

Role-Play Materials

- Toy telephone, full-length mirror
- Simple housekeeping equipment
- Simple doll equipment – carriage, bed

From around 1-1/2

- Simple dress-ups – hats, scarves, ties, shoes, jewelry
- Role-play toys that can be pushed and make noise – mower, vacuum
- Child-sized equipment – oven, fridge, sink, table and chairs

Play Scenes

(All figures should be at least 1-3/4 inches (44mm) in diameter, however if any object appears to fit easily in the child's mouth, **keep it away from the child)**

Before 1-1/2

- Child may enjoy handling, carrying around figures

From around 1-1/2

- Familiar, realistic scenes – farm, airport, garage – not overly detailed pieces (4-6 pieces).
- Prefer scenes with moving parts or that make noise

Transportation Toys

- Lightweight vehicles of a size for easy handling (not oo small) and with secure wheels
- Push or pull cars and trains
- Vehicles that make noise
- First train – 1-2 cars, no tracks, simple or no coupling system

From around 1-1/2

- More detailed vehicles – doors, hoods that open
- Trains with simple coupling system – large hooks, magnets

CREATIVE PLAY (arts, crafts, music)

Musical Instruments

- Rhythm instruments operated by shaking – enclosed bells, rattles

From around 1-1/2

- Rhythm instruments, operated by banging – symbols, drums, xylophones

Arts and Craft Materials

- Large crayons
- Sturdy large-size paper

Audio-Visual Equipment operated by adult

- Tapes, records or CDs of nursery rhymes and rhythms
- Hand-cranked music box, worked by child if crang is large and easy to turn

LEARNING PLAY

Books and "Peek-a-Boo" Books

- Sturdy cloth plastic, cardboard books with few pages
- Picture books, nursery rhymes, stories with repetition
- Books to be held and read by adult can be more fragile with paper pages

From around 1-1/2

- Touch-me or tactile books

OLDER TODDLERS (2 Year Olds)

ABILITIES AND INTEREST

PHYSICAL

- Skilled at most simple large muscle skills
- Lots of physical testing – jumping from heights, climbing, hanging by arms, rolling, galloping, somersaults, rough-and-tumble play
- Throws and retrieves all kinds of objects
- Pushes self on wheeled objects with good steering
- By 2-1/2 to 3 years, good hand and finger coordination
- Lots of active play with small objects – explores different qualities of play materials

MENTAL

- Interested in attributes of objects – texture, shape, size, color
- Can match a group of similar objects
- Plays with pattern, sequence, order of size
- First counting skills
- First creative activities (drawing, construction, clay) – process still more important than final product
- Beginning to solve problems in head
- Imaginative fantasy play increases – continued interest in domestic imitation

- Fantasy play alone or with adult – child also makes toys carry out actions on other toys

SOCIAL

- Main interest still in parents, but begins to play cooperatively with other children (especially 30 to 36 months)
- Uses language to express wishes to others
- Engages in game-like interactions with others – also some pretend play with others
- Enjoys hearing simple stories read from picture books, especially stories with repetition
- Strong desire for independence – shows pride in accomplishment

ALL TOYS

Beginning of cooperative social play

Increasing interest in pretend play

Love o f physical active play

Child prefers action toys, toys that produce movement or sounds by child's own efforts

More realism preferred

- Begins to pay attention to qualities of objects
- Prefers toys with working parts

Toys should be lightweight enough for easy lifting, carrying

Bright colors preferred

Toys should meet safety regulations for age

- Sturdy, unbreakable, not likely to break into small pieces and strong enough for child to stand on or in
- Nontoxic materials
- No sharp points or edges
- Too large to be lodged in windpipe, ears, nostrils
-
- No detachable small parts
- No parts that could pinch or entrap fingers, toes, hair
- Not put together with easily exposed straight pins, sharp wires, nails
- No electrical parts unless supervised by adult

ACTIVE PLAY

Push and Pull Toys

- Pull toys with strings
- Doll carriages
- Wagons
- Small, light wheel barrel
- interest in push toys that look like adult equipment – lawnmower, vacuum, shopping cart

Ride-On Toys

- interest in realistic-looking ride-ons – tractors, motorcycles
- ride-ons with storage trays or bins
- ride-ons propelled by bouncing up and down
- when children begin to pedal (around 2-1/2 – 3) small tricycle

Outdoor and Gym Equipment

- all gym equipment needs adult supervision
- tunnels

- climbing structures and slides
- stationary rather than moving outdoor equipment
- swings with curved, soft seats and restraining straps

Sports Equipment

- sleds sized to child (shorter length than child's height)
- spinning seat
- pool toys (tubes, mats) with adult supervision
- balls of all sizes, but especially large balls (All balls given to this age group should be at least 1-3/4 inches (44 mm) in diameter, however, if any object appears to fit easily in the child's mouth, **keep it away from the child.)**

MANIPULATIVE PLAY

Construction Toys

- solid, wooden unit bocks
- large, hollow building blocks (cardboard, wood, plastic)
- large plastic bricks (2-4 inches or 50-100mm) to be pressed together
- plastic interlocking rings, large plastic nuts and bolts

Puzzles

- fit-in puzzle
- *2 to 2-1/2 years, 4-5 pieces*
- *2 -1/2 to 3 years, 6-12 pieces*
- Puzzles with knobs easier (knobs should be firmly attached)

Pattern-Making Toys

- Peg boards with large pegs

- Color cubes
- Magnetic boards with shapes, animals, people
- Color forms (*from around 2-1/2*)

Manipulative Toys

- Fit-together toys of 5-10 pieces
- Nesting toys with multiple pieces, including barrel toys that require screwing motion
- Number/counting boards with large pegs
- Shape sorters with common shapes
- Pounding/hammering toys
- Smelling jars
- Feel bag or box
- Color/picture dominoes
- Simple lotto matching games based on color, pictures

Dressing, Lacing, Stringing Toys

- Large colored beads (All beads given to this age group should be at least 1-3/4 inches (44 mm) in diameter, however, if any object appears to fit easily in the child's mouth, **keep it away from the child**)
- Lacing card or wooden shoe for lacing
- Dressing books and dolls
- Frames, cubes for lacing, buttoning, snapping, hooking

Sand and Water Play Toys (with Adult Supervision)

- Bathtub activity centers
- Nesting tub toys
- Tub toys with removable figures, accessories
- Linking tub toys
- Small boats (no metal parts)
- Small and large sandbox tools (with blunt edges)
- Water/sand mills

- Sprinklers

MAKE-BELIEVE PLAY

Dolls

- Soft-bodied and rubber baby dolls
- More realistic dolls with hair and moving eyes
- Dolls to fit in child's arms, also small realistic dolls
- Talking dolls operated by pulling string
- Large peg dolls
- Doll accessories – simple and sturdy
- Caretaking accessories – bottle, blanket
- Simple removable garments (hook and loop, large snap fasteners)

Stuffed Toys

- Soft pliable animals
- Mother and baby combinations
- Preference for realistic animals, replicas of familiar characters
- Toys with music box inside

Puppets

- Small hand puppets (hand-and-arm puppets too large)
- Lightweight, sized to fit child's hand
- Puppets doubling as stuffed toys
- Puppets representing familiar characters

Role-Play Materials

- Dress-ups and costumes
- Equipment should be realistic looking
- Child-sized equipment – stove, cooking board, refrigerator
- Doll equipment
- All housekeeping equipment – cleaning sets, pots and pans, bath and laundry
- Toys that can be pushed – vacuum, lawnmower, shopping cart
- Full length mirror
-

Play Scenes

- Familiar, realistic-looking scenes – farm, garage, airport
- Scenes with multiple pieces but not highly detailed
- Preference for moving parts, parts that make noise
- Interior of scenes easily accessible
- Vehicle sets with figures

Transportation Toys

- Small, realistic cars (not metal)
- Vehicles with moving parts
- Large trucks (metal too heavy) – moving parts, parts operated by large lever (with knob on end)
- cars, trucks with removable figures, accessories
- small trains with sample coupling mechanism – no tracks

CREATIVE PLAY

Musical Instruments

- all rhythm instruments – belts, rattles, cymbals, drums, triangle, rhythm stick, sand blocks, xylophones
- horns and whistles (*around 2-1/2*)

Art and Craft Materials

- large crayons
- non-toxic paints (finger and tempera) and short handled brushes with blunt ends
- clay
- sturdy markers
- blunt end scissors
- chalkboard, large chalk
- colored construction paper

Audio-Visual Equipment

- operated by adult, tapes, records, CDs
- hand cranked music box if crank is large and easy to turn

LEARNING PLAY

Games

- lotto matching games based on color pictures
- dominoes, especially giant dominoes
- board games based on chance – only a few large pieces or pairs

Specific Skill Development Toys

Simple teaching toys for

- matching/sorting, shapes, colors, letters/sounds, numbers, concepts
- all electrically powered toys need adult supervision

BOOKS

- sturdy books with heavy paper, cardboard pages
- short simple stories with repetition and familiar subjects
- simple pictures with clear color, few details
- pop-up books
- hidden picture books
- dressing books

PRESCHOOLERS, 3, 4 AND 5 YEARS

ABILITIES AND INTERESTS

PHYSICAL

- Runs, jumps, climbs, balances with assurance – by 5, gross motor skills are well developed
- Likes risks; tests of physical strength and skill – loves acrobatics and outdoor equipment
- Increasing finger control – can pick up small objects, cut on a line with scissors, hold pencil in adult grasp, string small beads (most children in this age group can begin using toys with smaller components. If child is still mouthing objects, select toys without small parts)
- Expert builder – loves small construction materials and also vigorous activity with big blocks, large construction materials
- By 5, rudimentary interest in ball games with simple rules and scoring

MENTAL

- Familiar with common shapes, primary colors
- Interest in simple number activities, alphabet play, copying letters, matching/sorting
- By 5, sorts and matches using more than one quality at a time

- Around 4 beings to be purposeful and goal-directed, to make us of a plan
- Interest in producing designs, including puzzles and in constructing play worlds
- First representational pictures
- Prefers realism
- Interest in nature, science, animals, time, how things work
- Peak interest in dramatic play – recreates adult occupations, uses costumes and props

SOCIAL

- Beginning to share and take turns, learning concept of fair play
- By 5, play is cooperative, practical, conforming
- Not ready for competitive play because hates to lose
- Enjoys simple board games based on chance, not strategy
- More sex differentiation in play roles, interests
- Enjoys looking at books and listening to stories from books

ALL TOYS

Preschoolers prefer toys with realistic detail and working parts

Increasing interest in dramatic and pretend play, by age 5, peak period for dramatic play, with all sorts of props

Period of peak interest in puppet play

Increasing construction activity, often with plan or goal

Period of peak interest in play scenes, small figures and cars

Most children in this age group can begin using toys with smaller components. If child is still mouthing objects, select toys without small parts

Toys should be sturdy

- Not likely to break easily into small pieces or leave jagged edges
- No sharp points or edges
- Not made of glass or brittle plastic '

Toys should be of nontoxic materials

Toys should have no electrical parts unless supervised by adult

ACTIVE PLAY

Push and Pull Toys

- Small wagons
- Small wheel barrel
- Push toys resembling adult tools – lawnmowers, vacuum, shopping cart
- Doll carriages and strollers

From age 5

- Full size wagons, scooters

Ride on Toys

- Tricycles sized to child
- 3 and 4 wheel pedal toys
- Vehicles and steering mechanisms
- Prefer realistic detailed vehicles
- Full-size rocking horse

From age 4

- Low-slung tricycles
- Battery-operated ride-ons

From age 5

- *Small bicycle with training wheels and footbrakes, sized to child*
- *Bicycle helmet*

OUTDOOR GYM EQUIPMENT

- Adult supervision recommended for gym equipment
- Stationary outdoor climbing equipment
- Slides (with side rails) and ladders
- Swings with curved, soft seats
- Balance board

From age 4

- Equipment with movable parts, small seesaws, hanging rings
- Swings with flat seats, plastic or rubber belts
- Rope ladders and ropes
- Gym sets with enclosures for pretend house or fort

SPORTS EQUIPMENT

- Ball of all shapes, sizes (If child is still mouthing objects, any object that appears to fit easily in the child's mouth **keep it away from the child**
- Double blade ice skates
- Sleds size graded (no handbrakes of steering mechanisms)

From age 4

- Lightweight soft baseball and bat
- Junior-sized soccer ball, football
- Speed-graded roller skates (plastic wheels, no ball bearings for reduced speed
- Kites
- Wading pool

From age 5

- Jump ropes
- Skis (sized to child).
- Flying disks (especially lightweight ones)
- Flat nosed magnetic or Velcro darts
- Inner tubes, kickboards, mattresses for beginning swimmers (adult supervision needed)

MANIPULATIVE PLAY

Construction Toys

- Solid wood unit blocks – large and small
- Large hollow blocks
- Most types of interlocking building systems, pieces of all sizes (plastic rather than metal pieces)
- No motorized parts
- Prefer sets that make realistic models
- Can connect pieces in specific order to create simple models

Puzzles

- Fit-in or framed puzzles *age 3*, up to 20 pieces, *age 4*, 20-30 pieces, *age 5*, up to 50 pieces
- Large, simple jigsaw puzzles (10-25 pieces)
- Number or letter puzzles, puzzle clocks
- Cardboard puzzles

Pattern-Making Toys

- Bead stringing – longer, thinner string with stiff tip), large beads (If child is still mouthing objects, any object that

- appears to fit easily in the child's mouth should be kept away from the child)
- Peg board with small pegs
- Color cubes/color forms
- Magnetic boards with shapes

From age 4

Beginning interest in design materials – mosaic blocks, felt boards, can follow, copy simple sequence

From age 5

Simple weaving (looper & heddle loom) small beads to string (1/2 in.) block printing equipment

Manipulative Toys

- Matching toys by color, shape or picture, *from age 4* by concept, letters (ABC), numbers (1-10)
- Sorting toys, number rods
- Number boards with smaller pegs
- Simple counting toys, lock boxes
- Nesting toys with multiple pieces and screw closing

From age 4

Geometrical concept toys

From age 5

Simple models of mechanical devices or natural objects, more complex lotto matching toys

Dressing, Lacing Stringing Toys

Frames/cards to button, hook, tie

From age 5

Simple sewing kits with thick cloth and blunt needle (with supervision)

Sand and Water Play Toys

- Large and small sandbox tools, bubbles
- Wind-up bath toys, bath activity centers

From age 4

- Sand molds, water pump
- Realistic working models of boats (no sharp metal parts)

MAKE BELIEVE PLAY

Dolls

- Realistic dolls with detail and accessories, especially baby dolls
- Dolls with hair, moving eyes, movable limbs, special Features

From age 5

- Child-proportioned dolls (can dress dolls if garments and fastenings are simple)
- Paper dolls to be punched out

Stuffed Toys

- Stuffed toys with accessories – ribbons, bells, simple clothes
- Realistic-looking toys – replicas of famous characters
- Music box toys

From age 5

Hand and arm puppets, more detailed puppets, puppets with limbs

Role-Play Materials

- Dress-ups costumes of all types
- Realistic detailed equipment – by 5 want it to really work
- Housekeeping and cooking equipment
- Toy telephone, toy camera, doctor kits
- Military costumes and props
- Specialized doll equipment
- Cash register, equipment to play store
- Play stages, large mirror

Play Scenes

- Scenes with a variety of realistic accessories and working parts
- Favorite themes – garage, farm, airport, space, fort
- Action/adventure sets, action figures
- First doll house – simple, few rooms, easy access, space to move objects around, sturdy furnishings

From age 5

- Can manipulate very small pieces, attention to realistic detail

Transportation Toys

- Toy cars of all sizes – small metal cars, trucks with very realistic detail
- Large-scale trucks, road machinery that really works (dumps, digs)
- Action/adventure vehicle sets
- Small, realistic trains

From age 5

Small trains with tracks, can work most train coupling systems, can plan, build simple track layouts, wind-up and spring driven cars

Projectile Toys – *none before age 4*

- Soft, flexible projectiles
- Action figures with projectile weapons

From age 5

- Guns shooting ping pong or foam balls, soft darts

CREATIVE PLAY (arts, crafts, music)

Musical Instruments

- All rhythm instruments
- Xylophones
- Instruments that require blowing – harmonica, horns, whistles, simple recorder
- Wind-up music boxes
- Piano – one finger tunes

Art and Craft Materials

From age 3

- Large crayons with many colors
- Color paddles
- Magic markers
- Finger and tempera paint
- Adjustable easel
- Brushes of various sizes
- Clay including modeling clay and tools
- Chalkboards and chalk of various sizes
- Scissors with rounded ends
- Paste and glue
- Sample block printing equipment
- Pop-it beads
- Large beads to string
- Simple sewing kits (without needles) until age 5

From age 4

- Increased interest in art products also can copy order
- Workbench, hammer, nails and saw with supervision

From age 5

- Smaller crayons, coloring books, water color paints, simple weaving loom, small beads to string, sewing kits with large blunt needles

Audio-Visual Equipment

- Hand-cranked music boxes
- Parent operated record tape and CD player

From age 4

- Record and tape players for child to operate
- Simple video games

From age 5

- Radio

LEARNING PLAY

- Pool toys (tubes, mats) with adult supervision

Games

- Dominoes (color or numbers)
- Simple matching and lotto games based on color, pictures
- Simple card games
- Bingo (picture)

From age 4

- First board games, based completely on chance – games should have few rules, simple scoring, no reading required beyond ABC, only a few pieces
- Games requiring simple fine motor coordination(picking up or balancing objects)

Specific Skills Development Toys

Simple electronic and other teaching toys for

- Matching/sorting
- Shapes and colors
- Numbers and letters

From age 4

- Simple computer programs for teaching color matching, letters classification numbers, sounds
- Simple science model

From age 5

- Science materials – magnets, flashlight, shells and rocks, magnifying glass, stethoscope, prism, aquarium, terrarium
- Clock
- Printing set
- Toy typewriter or computer
- Simple calculator
- Computer programs to teach simple programming

Books

- Picture books, simple stories, rhymes
- Complex pop-up books
- Like complex illustrations with an abundance of detail

Age 3 interests

- Here-and-now stories
- Animal stories
- Alphabet books
- Words and rhymes

Age 4 interests

- Wild stories, silly humor
- Information books
- Familiar places, people

Age 5 interests

- Realistic stories
- Poetry
- Primers
- Animals who behave like people

For further information, write
U.S. Consumer Product Safety Commission
Washington D.C. 20207

To report a product hazard or a product-related injury, write to the U.S. Consumer Product Safety Commission, Washington, D.C. 20207, or call the toll free hotline 1-800-638-82772. A teletypewriter for the hearing and speaking impaired is available on 1-800-638-8270

www.ingramcontent.com/pod-product-compliance
Lightning Source LLC
Chambersburg PA
CBHW080937040426
42443CB00015B/3455